D0118765

CONTINENTS OF THE WORLD
NORTH AMERICA

Garrett Nagle

WORLD ALMANAC® LIBRARY

Please visit our web site at: www.worldalmanaclibrary.com
For a free color catalog describing World Almanac® Library's list of high-quality books
and multimedia programs, call 1-800-848-2928 (USA) or 1-800-387-3178 (Canada).
World Almanac® Library's fax: (414) 332-3567.

Library of Congress Cataloging-in-Publication Data

Nagle, Garrett.
    North America / by Garrett Nagle.
       p. cm. — (Continents of the world)
    Includes bibliographical references and index.
    ISBN 0-8368-5914-6 (lib. bdg.)
    ISBN 0-8368-5921-9 (softcover)   3656 7807 9/07
    1. North America—Juvenile literature. I. Title. II. Continents of the
world (Milwaukee, Wis.)
    E38.5.N34   2005
    970—dc22   2005041600

This North American edition first published in 2006 by
World Almanac® Library
330 West Olive Street, Suite 100
Milwaukee, WI 53212 USA

Commissioning editor: Victoria Brooker
Editor: Kelly Davis
Inside design: Jane Hawkins
Series concept and project management by
EASI-Educational Resourcing, (info@easi-er.co.uk)
Statistical research: Anna Bowden
World Almanac® Library editor: Barbara Kiely Miller
World Almanac® Library art direction: Tammy West
World Almanac® Library cover design: Dave Kowalski
World Almanac® Library production: Jessica Morris

Photo credits: Bridgeman Art Library/Private Collection 8; Corbis: cover, 1, 17 (Tom Bean), 2 (David
Muench), 5 (Tom Brakefield), 6 (Free Agents Limited), 7 (Greg Probst), 9, 10 (Bettmann), 11 (Peter
Guttman), 12 (John Van Hasselt/Corbis Sygma), 13 (Peter Turnley/The Denver Post), 14 (Jonathan Blair),
16 (Annie Griffiths Belt), 18 (Alan Schein Photography), 19 (Kevin Fleming), 20 (Henry Romero/Reuters),
21 (Paul A. Souders), 23 (Ed Kashi), 24 (Robert Estall), 25 (Chuck Savage), 26 (Najlah Feanny/Corbis
Saba), 27 (Bruce Adams); Eye Ubiquitous 28 (Bob Krist), 29 (Jeremy Horner), 31 (John and Lisa Merrill),
32(t) (Macduff Everton), 32(b) (Gary Hershorn/Reuters); 33 (Tim Thompson), 34 (Jacques
Pavlovsky/Corbis Sygma), 35 (Peter Yates), 36 (David Zimmerman), 37 (Reuters), 38 (Gunter Marx
Photography), 39 (Reuters), 40 (Robert Semeniuk), 41 (Tim Thompson), 42 (Ed Kashi), 44 (Annie
Griffiths Belt), 45 (Owen Franken), 46 (Jonathan Blair), 48 (Erik De Castro/Reuters), 49 (Reuters), 50
(Bill Gentile), 51 (Juan Carlos Ulate/ Reuters), 52 (Kennan Ward), 53 (W. Perry Conway), 54 (Raymond
Gehman), 55 (Macduff Everton), 56 (Stephen Frink), 57 (Macduff Everton), 59 (Bob Krist); Getty Images
47 (Stone). Maps and graphs: Martin Darlison, Encompass Graphics. Population Density Map © 2003
UT-Battelle, LLC.

Printed in China

1 2 3 4 5 6 7 8 9 09 08 07 06 05

**Badlands National Park, South Dakota,
in the United States.**

CONTENTS

NORTH AMERICA — A CONTINENT OF CONTRASTS

North America is a huge and spectacular continent and one of the most varied. It is the third largest continent after Asia and Africa, covering about 9,341,000 square miles (24,200,000 square kilometers)—about twice the size of Europe. North America includes Greenland (a self-governing territory of Denmark) and the

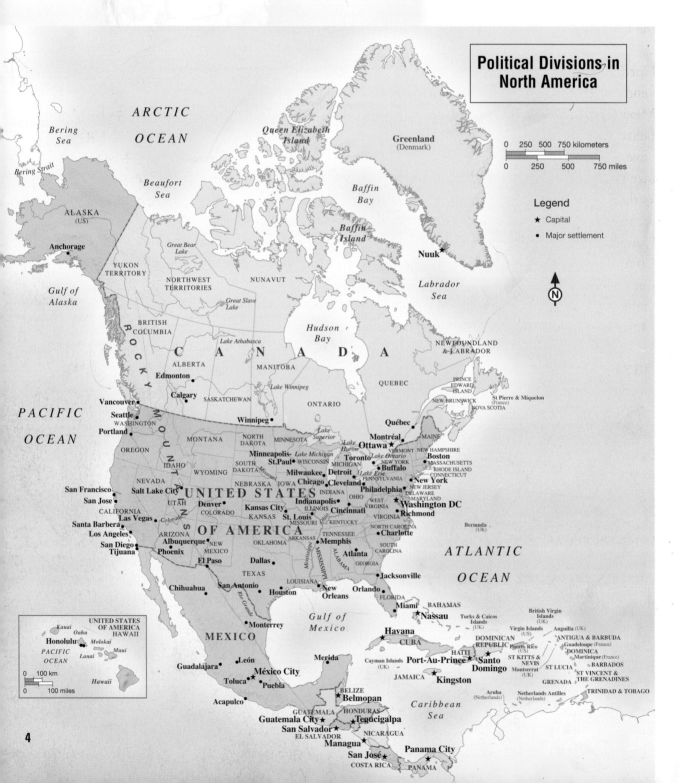

Political Divisions in North America

ARCTIC OCEAN

Bering Sea

Bering Strait

Beaufort Sea

Queen Elizabeth Island

Greenland (Denmark)

Baffin Bay

Baffin Island

ALASKA (US)

Anchorage

Gulf of Alaska

YUKON TERRITORY

Great Bear Lake

NORTHWEST TERRITORIES

NUNAVUT

Nuuk ★

Labrador Sea

0 250 500 750 kilometers
0 250 500 750 miles

Legend
★ Capital
• Major settlement

BRITISH COLUMBIA

Great Slave Lake

Lake Athabasca

Hudson Bay

C A N A D A

NEWFOUNDLAND & LABRADOR

Edmonton

Calgary

ALBERTA

SASKATCHEWAN

MANITOBA

Lake Winnipeg

QUEBEC

St Pierre & Miquelon (France)

PRINCE EDWARD ISLAND

NEW BRUNSWICK NOVA SCOTIA

Vancouver

Seattle

WASHINGTON

Portland

PACIFIC OCEAN

R O C K Y   M O U N T A I N S

Winnipeg

ONTARIO

Québec

Montréal

Ottawa ★

MAINE

NEW HAMPSHIRE

Lake Superior

OREGON

MONTANA

NORTH DAKOTA

MINNESOTA

IDAHO

SOUTH DAKOTA

WYOMING

Lake Michigan

Lake Huron

Minneapolis-St.Paul

WISCONSIN

Milwaukee

MICHIGAN

Detroit

Toronto

Lake Ontario

Buffalo

Lake Erie

VERMONT

NEW YORK

Boston

MASSACHUSETTS

RHODE ISLAND

CONNECTICUT

NEBRASKA

IOWA

Chicago

ILLINOIS

INDIANA

Cleveland

OHIO

PENNSYLVANIA

New York

NEW JERSEY

DELAWARE

San Francisco

San Jose

NEVADA

Salt Lake City

UTAH

Denver

COLORADO

Kansas City

KANSAS

Indianapolis

St. Louis

MISSOURI

Cincinnati

Philadelphia

MARYLAND

Washington DC

Richmond

WEST VIRGINIA

VIRGINIA

U N I T E D   S T A T E S

CALIFORNIA

Santa Barbera

Las Vegas

Colorado

KENTUCKY

Bermuda (UK)

Los Angeles

San Diego

Tijuana

ARIZONA

O F   A M E R I C A

Albuquerque

NEW MEXICO

Phoenix

OKLAHOMA

ARKANSAS

TENNESSEE

NORTH CAROLINA

Charlotte

SOUTH CAROLINA

El Paso

Dallas

TEXAS

Mississippi

MISSISSIPPI

ALABAMA

GEORGIA

Memphis

Atlanta

ATLANTIC OCEAN

Chihuahua

San Antonio

Rio Grande

Houston

LOUISIANA

New Orleans

Orlando

Jacksonville

FLORIDA

Miami

BAHAMAS

Nassau ★

Turks & Caicos Islands (UK)

British Virgin Islands (UK)

Virgin Islands (US)

Anguilla (UK)

Monterrey

Gulf of Mexico

Havana ★

CUBA

DOMINICAN REPUBLIC

Puerto Rico (US)

ANTIGUA & BARBUDA

Guadeloupe (France)

MEXICO

Merida

Cayman Islands (UK)

Port-Au-Prince ★

HAITI

Santo Domingo ★

ST KITTS & NEVIS

Montserrat (UK)

DOMINICA

Martinique (France)

ST LUCIA

BARBADOS

Guadalajara

León

México City ★

Toluca

Puebla

JAMAICA

Kingston ★

Aruba (Netherlands)

Netherlands Antilles (Netherlands)

GRENADA

ST VINCENT & THE GRENADINES

TRINIDAD & TOBAGO

Acapulco

BELIZE

Belmopan ★

Caribbean Sea

GUATEMALA

HONDURAS

Guatemala City ★

Tegucigalpa ★

San Salvador ★

EL SALVADOR

NICARAGUA

Managua ★

San José ★

Panama City ★

COSTA RICA

PANAMA

UNITED STATES OF AMERICA HAWAII

Kauai

Oahu

Honolulu

Molokai

PACIFIC OCEAN

Lanai

Maui

0 100 km
0 100 miles

Hawaii

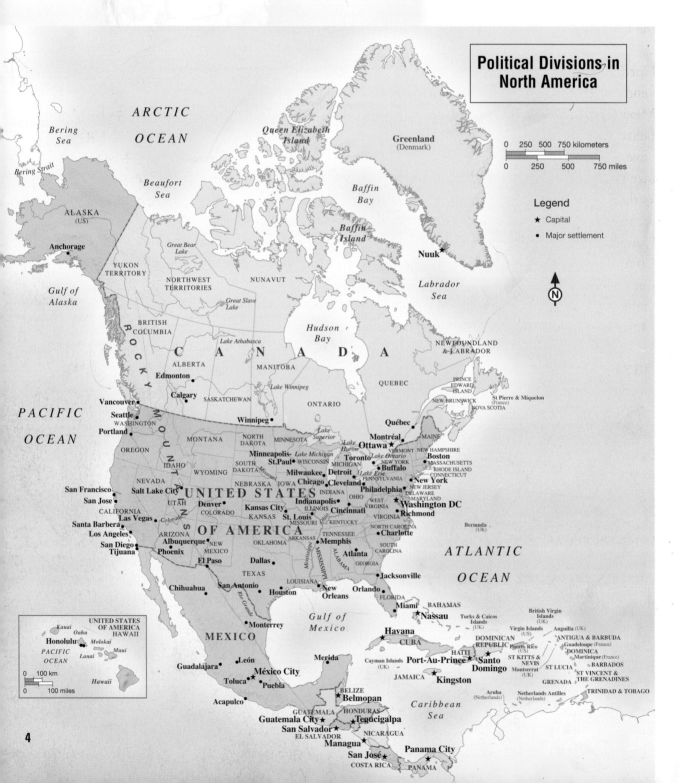

countries of Canada, the United States, and Mexico. For the purposes of this book, the islands of the Caribbean and the countries of Central America as far south as Panama are also considered to be part of North America because of their close geographical, economic, and political ties with Mexico, the United States, and Canada.

North America contains twenty-three independent countries. The United States and Mexico are both federal republics. Canada, Belize, and eight Caribbean countries each have their own governments, but they recognize the British monarch, Queen Elizabeth II, as their head of state. The continent has ten democratic republics, including Costa Rica, Panama, and Trinidad and Tobago, and one Communist republic, Cuba. Fourteen territories connected to Britain, France, the United States, and Denmark, such as Greenland and Martinique, are also included in the region.

PHYSICAL VARIETY

North America boasts the world's largest island, Greenland, which is 836,109 square miles (2,166,086 sq km) in area, as well as Lake Superior—the biggest freshwater lake in the world. Lake Superior is one of the five Great Lakes, which, along with their many connected rivers and waterways, account for one-fifth of the world's freshwater. In the United States, one of the world's most famous and spectacular natural features, the Grand Canyon, reaches a depth of 1 mile (1.6 kilometers). Running from north to south, the Western Cordillera is a vast mountain range that stretches from Alaska all the way to Panama in Central America. In Canada and the United States, this range

is known as the Rocky Mountains, or "the Rockies." In Mexico and Central America, it is called the Sierra Madre.

A WEALTH OF WILDLIFE

North America's many differing landscapes offer habitats for a wide variety of wildlife. The continent is home to many well-known mammals, including grizzly bears and coyotes, and birds such as the bald eagle and the rare Californian condor. Many exotic species also make their home here, including jaguars in Central America, howler monkeys in Barbados, and the Cuban pygmy frog. Belize's coral reef is the world's fifth largest and supports a great diversity of marine life. Many of the species in Central America and the Caribbean, however, are vulnerable to extinction or are critically endangered, largely due to population growth, urbanization, and farming.

The jaguar is one of the most beautiful—and dangerous—mammals living in the Belize rain forest.

1. THE HISTORY OF NORTH AMERICA

*T*HE EARLIEST PEOPLE TO SEE THE LAND THAT IS NOW NORTH America probably came from Asia about 15,000 years ago. At that time, Earth was experiencing an Ice Age, and such a large amount of water was locked into huge ice sheets that sea levels were about 575 feet (175 meters) lower than today. It is generally believed that the Bering Strait—a narrow passage in the far north that separates North America and Asia—was not covered by sea during that time, creating a land bridge between the two continents.

This pyramid at Kukulcan is just one of the many Mayan sites found across much of Central America.

EARLY SETTLERS

These early peoples were hunters and gatherers, and they gradually moved south to warmer climates. In some places, they began to settle and grow food. They are believed to be the ancestors of most Native Americans. One exception is the Inuit of the far north. The Inuit are believed to have descended from Asian ancestors who had adapted to living in very cold climates, hunting caribou (reindeer), seals, and even whales. They probably traveled by boats along the coastlines of the Arctic Ocean about 5,000 years ago. Instead of moving south, they traveled east and eventually settled in Greenland. The Inuit still live in parts of Alaska, Canada, and Greenland.

FACT FILE

The term *Inuit* refers to the people inhabiting the Arctic coast of North America. The term *eskimo*, which means "eater of raw meat," is now considered offensive.

CENTRAL AMERICA AND THE CARIBBEAN

Some groups of people settled in the Caribbean and Central America. The Arawak, for example, were found on most of the Caribbean islands. They practiced shifting cultivation, a type of farming in which farmers grow crops on a piece of land until it is no longer productive, then abandon the land and move on to a new area. In about 1300, the Arawak were driven out of many Caribbean islands by the Carib, who came from the northern coast of South America.

On mainland Central America, the Maya Indians lived in the Yucatán Peninsula of Mexico beginning about 2600 B.C. They spread into Guatemala, Belize, and western Honduras. Another important people, the Aztecs, migrated from northern Mexico into the Valley of Mexico in the 1100s. In 1325, the Aztecs began to reclaim lake marshland to build their capital on the site occupied today by Mexico City.

VIKINGS

Even during this early period of settlement, there was a European presence in North America. About the middle of the tenth century, Vikings from Denmark, Sweden, and Norway built settlements and traded along Canada's coastline between

Newfoundland and Baffin Island. They used wood from Newfoundland to build boats and houses in Greenland.

The remains of the first Viking settlement in Newfoundland are found at L'Anse aux Meadows National Historic Site.

THE COLONIAL PERIOD

Europeans began settling in North America in the late 1400s and early 1500s. Britain, France, Spain, and Portugal were all eager to exploit North America's reputed resources and to control territories in the "New World," as it became known.

veyothpan . oncā qnamicq3 mtlatoque q̄maca q̄yxq̄ch qualom .

Aztecs present gifts to the Spanish *conquistador*, Hernán Cortés, who later conquered the Aztec Empire.

Explorers from Spain reached the Caribbean in 1492 and Central America in 1501. Spanish *conquistadors*, or conquerors, invaded Central America and fought the Native peoples. By 1525, the Spanish controlled much of the region. The conquistadors also brought with them diseases, such as smallpox and measles, which were previously unknown in North America. The Native peoples had no immunity to these diseases, and within one hundred years, nearly 90 percent of the indigenous (native) population in the Caribbean and Central America had been wiped out by disease.

French and British settlers began to arrive along the coasts of present-day Canada and the United States beginning in about 1600. A permanent settlement was established in Virginia in 1607 and came to be known as Jamestown. The settlement at Jamestown became profitable for a reason that nobody had foreseen—tobacco. This plant was grown widely by Native Americans, and they introduced it to the Europeans. First used as an important medicine, tobacco quickly became a valuable cash crop in Virginia, with most of the crop being exported to Britain.

INDEPENDENCE AND MANIFEST DESTINY

In 1775, thirteen American colonies went to war against Britain. Many American colonists resented the high taxes that Britain imposed on them, particularly because they had no representation in the British parliament. In 1776, the colonists issued a Declaration of Independence, marking the birth of the United States of America. The war, known as the American Revolutionary War, continued until 1783, when Britain finally recognized the new country.

Ever since the arrival of the first Europeans, relations between settlers and Native Americans had been uneasy and, sometimes, hostile. As the United States expanded during the 1800s, a philosophy known as Manifest Destiny was often used to justify

• • • • • • ▶ IN FOCUS: Slavery and the Civil War

Black people from Africa were originally brought to North America to work as slaves on plantations. The slave trade from Africa to the Caribbean and the United States brought some 13–14 million Africans to the region in the 1700s. Slavery became a vital part of the economies of the Caribbean and the southern states of the United States. In these regions, slaves provided the labor force for plantations growing cotton, sugar, and tobacco.

During the 1800s, the issue of slavery caused the United States to split in two. Many people in the richer, industrial north became opposed to slavery and called for its abolition. People in the southern states, however,

wanted to defend their prosperous, agricultural way of life—which was dependent on slavery. Starting in 1860, the southern states formally withdrew from the Union to form the Confederate States of America. Fighting between Union and Confederate forces began in 1861. The bitter and bloody Civil War lasted for four years. It ended with victory for the Union forces and the abolition of slavery throughout the country.

A slave family at work on a cotton plantation near Savannah, Georgia, in the southeastern United States.

the treatment of Native Americans. The idea of Manifest Destiny was that white Americans had the right to spread across and possess the continent of North America—even if this meant killing Native Americans or forcing them off their lands.

CHANGE AND REVOLUTION IN CENTRAL AMERICA

Spanish rule in Central America came to an end in the 1820s. The United Provinces of Central America was formed in 1823, but by 1839, this union had split into the independent states of Guatemala, Honduras, El Salvador, Nicaragua, and Costa Rica. Throughout much of the twentieth century, these states had numerous internal disputes, experiencing military takeovers as well as civil wars. Since the 1980s, however, there has been a general trend toward democratically elected governments.

Nicaragua, for example, experienced more than four decades of dictatorship under the Somoza family. This rule came to an end in 1978 with the Sandinista Revolution. Eleven years of civil war followed between the Sandinistas and their opponents, the Contras—former members of the National Guard who had supported the Somoza regime. The Contras were backed by the United States, which was suspicious about the close links between the Sandinistas and the Communist regime in Cuba and which wanted to destabilize the Sandinista government.

The Contras finally disbanded in 1990. Although the Sandinistas won democratic elections in 1985, they were defeated in 1990, 1996, and 2001. Since 1990, Nicaragua has been politically stable. Its fragile economy, however, shattered by years of civil war, received a further setback when the country was badly hit by Hurricane Mitch in 1998.

FACT FILE

Between 1979 and 1991, civil war in El Salvador claimed the lives of more than 75,000 people.

Sandinista rebels arrive in the capital of Nicaragua, Managua, to take control of the government on June 20, 1979.

INDEPENDENCE IN THE CARIBBEAN

During the global economic depression of the 1930s, the Caribbean islands experienced high levels of unemployment. Demands for independence were urged by labor movements on many of the islands. The British responded by allowing self-government; the French incorporated their islands more closely into the French economy; and the Dutch permitted more self-rule.

After World War II, Britain tried to be free of its responsibilities to its Caribbean colonies by creating a single federal state—the West Indies Federation—which represented dozens of islands scattered over 1,990 miles (3,200 km) of ocean. Jamaica was the first island to leave the Federation in 1961, followed soon after by Trinidad. Both islands became independent states in 1962. Barbados gained independence in 1966, and the other smaller islands, such as Dominica, Grenada, and St. Kitts, gradually followed suit.

Jamaica was the first British colony to become independent in 1962, an event commemorated in the annual Independence Day Parade in Charlestown.

CANADA

Canada remains part of the British Commonwealth, but separatist movements exist within Canada. In 1976, for example, French Canadians gained control of the province of Québec. The following year, a law was passed making French the official language of the province. In 1992, a self-governing homeland for the Inuit population was approved, and in 1999, that territory, Nunavut, was established out of the Northwest Territories.

FACT FILE

Nunavut, the Inuit homeland established in 1999, covers nearly one-quarter of Canada's land area.

The explosion of the atomic bomb at Hiroshima, Japan, on August 6, 1945. Three days later, the United States dropped another atomic bomb on the Japanese city of Nagasaki.

FACT FILE

Hawaii was annexed by the United States in 1898 and became a U.S. territory in 1900, thereby making all of its residents U.S. citizens. In 1959, Hawaii became the fiftieth U.S. state.

THE UNITED STATES IN THE TWENTIETH CENTURY

During the twentieth century, the United States, Europe, large parts of Asia, and other Pacific Rim countries were involved in two devastating world wars. The United States entered World War I (1914–1918) in 1917, following the sinking of U.S. ships by German submarines. The United States became involved in World War II in 1941, after Japan bombed Pearl Harbor in Hawaii, the home of the U.S. Pacific naval fleet. The United States and its allies were victorious in the European fighting in May 1945. The end of the war in the Pacific came about four months later, with the surrender of Japan several days after the United States dropped atomic bombs on the Japanese cities of Hiroshima and Nagasaki.

For the next forty-five years, the United States and the Union of Soviet Socialist Republics (USSR), the world's two "superpowers," were engaged in an intense hostility and rivalry known as the cold war. This power struggle was a response by the United States and its Western allies to the spread and influence of Communism. Although the cold war was not a war in the usual sense, the United States did become involved in conflicts, such as the Korean War (1950–1953) and the Vietnam War (1964–1975). The cold war ended after the reunification of Germany, following the tearing down of the Berlin Wall in 1989 and the collapse of the political systems in many Communist countries, including the USSR (1991).

Opinions about the involvement of the United States in world affairs are divided. Critics debate whether the country has provided strong leadership or whether it has interfered in the

internal affairs of other countries, such as in conflicts in the Middle East, Bosnia, the Gulf states, and in Iraq. During the late twentieth and early twenty-first centuries, the United States has also been the target of terrorist attacks, both at home and abroad. People responsible for the attacks often believe that the United States does not have the right to be involved in making decisions that affect other countries and should not have a physical presence in them.

U.S. soldiers stand guard in Baghdad, the capital of Iraq, in 2003. Since 1945, the United States has played a major role in world affairs.

CUBA

In 1959, Cuban dictator Fulgencio Batista was overthrown in a revolution led by a young lawyer, Fidel Castro. Castro established a Communist government and seized U.S. businesses in Cuba, putting them under Cuban government control. In response, the United States banned trade with Cuba and cut off diplomatic relations. In 1962, there were reports that the Soviet Union was constructing nuclear missile launch sites in Cuba, capable of launching attacks on U.S. cities. The United States responded with a naval blockade of Cuba, demands that the launch sites be removed, and a threat of nuclear retaliation against the Soviet Union. During this crisis, the world stood on the edge of nuclear war, until the Soviet Union agreed to turn back ships carrying nuclear missiles to Cuba and to take down the launch-sites.

Cuba continued to receive aid from the Soviet Union until the collapse of Communism in the late 1980s and early 1990s, when the aid dried up. As trade with the former Soviet Union also slumped, Cuba's economy suffered greatly. In addition, Cuba is still subject to U.S. sanctions. Economic growth is slow (just over 1 percent in 2003) and is fueled mainly by tourism and from money sent back to Cuba from Cubans living abroad.

FACT FILE

In 2003, a total of about 2,500 Cubans attempted to leave Cuba for the United States by crossing the Straits of Florida in boats. The U.S. Coast Guard turned back about 60 percent of these people.

2. NORTH AMERICAN ENVIRONMENTS

NORTH AMERICA HAS A HUGE RANGE OF ENVIRONMENTS, FROM POLAR deserts to subtropical forests, from coastal coral to mangroves, from lofty mountain peaks to rolling grasslands. The continent contains islands with unique flora and fauna, as well as vast river networks and wetlands.

The Sierra Madre was formed by tectonic forces that pushed up the limestone strata into near vertical layers.

TECTONICS AND THE ENVIRONMENT

The movement of the plates that make up Earth's crust is known as plate tectonics. Tectonic movements have played a major role in the formation of some of the mountainous environments in North America. Where two plates meet, the denser plate plunges beneath, or subducts, the less dense plate and pushes the ground upward. This force has helped to create mountain ranges, such as the Rocky Mountains and the Sierra Madre, as well as the rugged Cordillera de Talamanca of Central America. Tectonic activity also explains the existence of volcanoes, such as Mount Saint Helens in the United States, Volcán Pacaya in Guatemala, and the Hawaiian Islands in the Pacific. Mount Saint Helens and Volcán Pacaya are situated on plate boundaries, where magma—molten rock from Earth's interior—breaks through to the surface. Magma can also rise to the surface underneath a plate, to form a hot spot. The Hawaiian Islands have been formed as the Pacific plate has moved slowly over a hot spot, creating a series of volcanoes.

FACT FILE

In Hawaii, the submarine volcano Loihi, which lies 3,280 feet (1,000 m) beneath the sea, is adding lava and building upward to become the next Hawaiian island—in about ten thousand years.

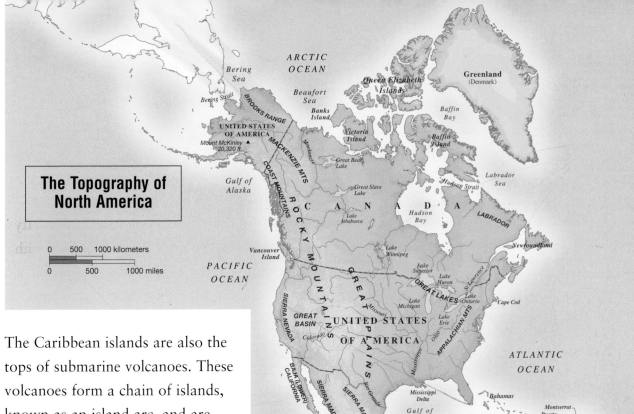

The Topography of North America

Legend
▲ Mountain

The Caribbean islands are also the tops of submarine volcanoes. These volcanoes form a chain of islands, known as an island arc, and are located along the zone where the North and South American plates collide with the Caribbean plate. The Caribbean has fifteen potentially active volcanoes. Some, such as Montserrat, are above ground while others, such as Kick 'em Jenny north of Grenada, are submerged beneath the sea. The volcanoes that form the oldest islands of the Caribbean—Jamaica, Hispaniola, and Cuba—are no longer active.

•••••• ▶ IN FOCUS: Living with the volcano

The eruption of the Soufriere Hills volcano on the island of Montserrat began in 1995. In 1997, clouds of superheated ash and gas, called pyroclastic flows, killed nineteen people and covered Plymouth (the capital city) in ash and mudflows. Montserrat's only airport was destroyed, and the southern half of the island was declared unsafe.

Since 2000, many people have returned to Montserrat to live, and much rebuilding has taken place in the northern part of the island. But volcanologists (people who study volcanoes) do not know whether the Soufriere Hills volcano will continue to erupt for another six—or six hundred—years!

FACT FILE

The largest earthquakes ever to affect North America were the three New Madrid earthquakes of 1811–1812, so-called because they were on a fault line near the town of New Madrid, Missouri. They measured at least 8.0 on the Richter Scale and caused large areas of the earth to sink, new lakes to form, and the Mississippi River to change its course.

FACT FILE

North America's highest point is Mount McKinley (Denali) in Alaska, at 20,320 feet (6,194 m).

The flat wheat fields of North Dakota are part of the Great Plains—the "bread-basket" of the world.

EARTHQUAKES

In some places, two plates slide horizontally against each other. A weakness in Earth's crust, usually at the edges of the plates, is called a fault line. The movement of the crust along a fault can cause both small and large earthquakes. The world's most famous fault line is the San Andreas Fault that runs through California for 700 miles (1,125 km). Notable earthquakes along this fault include the 1906 earthquake in San Francisco and the 1994 Northridge earthquake in Los Angeles, both of which brought great destruction. The 1906 earthquake registered more than 8.0 on the Richter scale; seven hundred people were killed; and much of San Francisco was destroyed by fire. In 1994, the earthquake measured 6.6 on the Richter scale; sixty people were killed; and damage was estimated at more than US$15 billion.

HIGH AND LOW LAND

North America has many dramatic mountains and areas of high elevation. More than half of Mexico is located 3,200 feet (1,000 m) above sea level. The Mexican plateau runs through the country from north to south. It forms a dry desert in the north, while further south the land rises and becomes more mountainous. The increase in altitude leads to a decrease in temperature, and the central highlands are about 18° Fahrenheit (10° Celsius) cooler than the northern desert. One-third of Central America is more than 3,200 feet (1,000 m) in height. The region has relatively few low-lying areas, but some of these are found along the Pacific and Caribbean coastlines, around lakes Nicaragua and Managua, and in the northern part of Guatemala. In the center of the United States and Canada are the central lowlands, which include the Great Plains. The central lowlands are bounded by higher ground. Toward the east are the Appalachian Mountains, characterized by low rounded ridges and gentle valleys, while the Rockies are in the west.

RIVERS AND LAKES

North America contains one of the world's largest and most important river basins. The Mississippi (2,340 miles/3,765 km) and Missouri (2,500 miles/4,023 km) rivers drain the area between the Appalachians and the Rockies—more than half of North America. The Mississippi and its valley are important for transportation, agriculture, and industry. The rivers on the western side of North America, such as the Columbia and Fraser rivers (which flow between the Western Cordillera range of mountains and the Pacific Ocean), are shorter in length but impressive in stature. Many of these rivers have eroded deep canyons, such as Fraser Canyon in British Columbia. The Colorado River cuts through the Rockies and continues into northern Arizona, where it has carved through rock more than 2,000 million years old to form the Grand Canyon. With a depth of 1 mile (1.6 km) from its rim, the Grand Canyon is 217 miles (350 km) long and 4–18 miles (6–29 km) wide. Canyons have become important locations for the building of large dams, a source of hydroelectric power. The lakes behind these dams are used as reservoirs and for recreation.

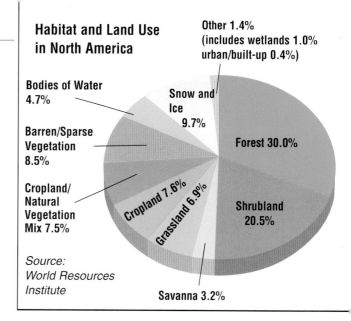

Habitat and Land Use in North America

- Other 1.4% (includes wetlands 1.0% urban/built-up 0.4%)
- Bodies of Water 4.7%
- Snow and Ice 9.7%
- Barren/Sparse Vegetation 8.5%
- Forest 30.0%
- Cropland/Natural Vegetation Mix 7.5%
- Cropland 7.6%
- Grassland 6.9%
- Shrubland 20.5%
- Savanna 3.2%

Source: World Resources Institute

Cape Solitude, Grand Canyon National Park, Arizona. The Colorado River has carved its way through rock to reveal 2,000 million years of geological history in the Grand Canyon.

Water rights have always been an important factor in the development of North America. There is an ongoing debate about whether freshwater from the Great Lakes should be made available to other areas and states outside the Great Lakes basin. An agreement known as Annex 2001 attempts to limit water usage from the lakes to local communities. Water rights are especially controversial in this part of North America because the Great Lakes are used for more than drinking water or irrigation. They are vital to the region's manufacturing, as well as its tourism and recreation.

Pressure to divert water outside the region is likely to come from the United States rather than Canada, because Canada has vast water resources on which to draw and a much smaller population than the United States.

Metropolitan Chicago overlooks Lake Michigan.

FACT FILE

The St. Lawrence River and the Great Lakes cover 94,600 square miles (245,000 sq km) and form a vast store of water that is a vital resource for drinking water, recreation, industry, transportation, and trade for large areas of the United States and Canada.

The group of five Great Lakes is another major natural feature that has an important economic function. Four of the Great Lakes—Superior, Huron, Erie, and Ontario—lie on the boundary between the United States and Canada, while one—Lake Michigan—is completely within the United States. The Great Lakes drain through the St. Lawrence River to the Gulf of St. Lawrence and the Atlantic Ocean.

WATER BOUNDARIES

Rivers and waterways help to mark the boundaries between the different countries of North America. Niagara Falls forms part of the boundary between the United States and Canada. The

American Falls are 167 feet (51 m) high and 1,083 feet (330 m) wide, while the Horseshoe Falls in Canada are 161 feet (49 m) high and 2,592 feet (790 m) wide. In Central America, the Rio Grande (1885 miles/3,034 km) flows along part of the boundary between the United States and Mexico, and the Usumacinta River (600 miles/965 km) is part of the border between Mexico and Guatemala.

The islands of the Caribbean have relatively short rivers. Some islands have very few rivers—notably Barbados, which is formed of permeable limestone but which has a substantial reservoir of groundwater beneath the surface that provides an important source of freshwater.

HUMAN IMPACT ON RIVERS AND LAKES

Humans have long manipulated rivers and lakes for their own gain. Rivers have been widened, straightened, deepened, dammed, and channeled. Engineering works on the Mississippi, for example, have shortened the river by 168 miles (270 km) by removing some of its meanders, or bends. In recent years, however, there has been a movement to restore some rivers to their natural state. The aim is to improve water quality by using vegetation and soil to filter pollutants from the water, as well as to allow floodplains to soak up flood waters. One example of this effort is the Kissimmee River in Florida, where over 39 square miles (100 sq km) of river and floodplain are being restored at a cost of over US$400 million. The first phase was completed in 2001, but the future of the project is uncertain due to a shortage of funding.

River engineers have reintroduced the historical meanders to the Kissimmee River in Florida.

CLIMATE AND WEATHER

The continent of North America stretches from the Arctic Circle almost to the equator. Combined with the influence of the continent's many different landscapes and the effects of the Pacific and Atlantic oceans, North America has an incredibly varied range of climates and temperatures.

Deep within the Arctic Circle, temperatures rise above the freezing point for only a few months of the year. In the Arctic, winter temperatures may be as low as −13° F (−25° C) and summer temperatures reach only 46° F (8° C). By contrast, in Cuba, the average temperature in January is as high as 70° F (21°C), and the average temperature in July is 86° F (30°C).

Rainfall across the continent is particularly varied. Areas that receive less than 10 inches (250 millimeters) of rain are termed deserts. North America has many desert areas, such as the Sonoran Desert in Mexico and Arizona and Death Valley in California. Cold deserts, such as Greenland, are also present. Rainfall is high along the Pacific coast of North America and also in Central America and the Caribbean. Much of the Caribbean, the countries of Central America, and the south and southeast coasts of the United States experience hurricanes and tropical storms between June and November. The driest parts of North America are in the interior.

A clear link exists between climate and ecosystems. In the far north, where conditions are coldest, tundra grasslands occur. Moving south, across much of southern Alaska and Canada, coniferous forests are found in areas that have significant snowfalls in winter but also warm summers.

FACT FILE

In 2004, three hurricanes, Charley, Frances, and Ivan, battered the Caribbean and the southeastern United States, causing more than forty deaths and extensive damage to Grenada, the Cayman Islands, Jamaica, Cuba, and Florida.

A flooded house on the coast of western Cuba takes a battering from Hurricane Ivan in 2004. Much of the Caribbean and the southern and eastern coasts of the United States are vulnerable to hurricane damage.

Broad-leaved, deciduous forests (which lose their leaves in winter) are found in warmer areas, such as northeastern United States, while grasslands flourish in the drier lands of the interior, such as the Great Plains. In southern California, Mediterranean conditions (warm, wet winters and hot, dry summers) produce Mediterranean woodland and chaparral, which is a type of Mediterranean shrub vegetation. In Central America and the Caribbean, the tropical climate is responsible for the rain forests that cover the region. The effect of the mountains in Costa Rica is to change the rain forest into cloud forest, as near-permanent clouds shroud the forest in mist.

The pattern of weather in North America appears to be changing. Increases in hurricane activity and strength, and changes in the El Niño circulation of ocean currents, may possibly be linked to global warming—the increase in temperatures throughout the world that is largely caused by the burning of fossil fuels. Any reduction in the burning of these valued fuels, however, may come at the expense of economic growth in North America.

Mount McKinley provides a stunning backdrop to this tundra landscape in Denali National Park, Alaska.

FACT FILE

Central parts of North America experience tornadoes that can have winds of up to 300 miles per hour (480 km/hour).

3. THE PEOPLE OF NORTH AMERICA

NORTH AMERICA HAS A POPULATION OF ABOUT 500 MILLION. ON THE whole, this continent is one of the most sparsely populated regions in the world, with an average of only 58.4 people per square mile (22.5/sq km)

DISTRIBUTION AND DENSITY

The distribution of population in North America is very uneven. Densities range from 1,533 people per square mile (598/sq km) in Barbados to 8 people per square mile (3/sq km) in Canada. More than half of the population of North America lives in the United States. In the U.S. states of Massachusetts and Connecticut, densities are more than 256 people per square mile (100/sq km), whereas in Colorado and New Mexico there are generally fewer than 26 people per square mile (10/sq km). Some areas have a very high population density. Los Angeles, California, and Mexico City, Mexico, for example, are known for their urban sprawl. In addition, some cities in the southern and western United States are among the fastest growing in North America, in some part thanks to a trend for people to move to warmer areas. Rapidly expanding cities are located in Nevada, Arizona, and California, particularly in cities where there is a concentration of high-tech industry, such as in San Jose, California, and Phoenix, Arizona.

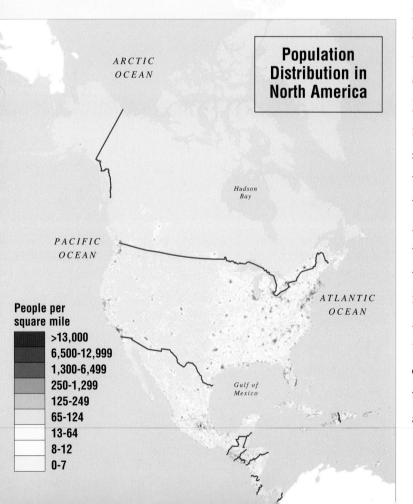

Population Distribution in North America

ARCTIC OCEAN

Hudson Bay

PACIFIC OCEAN

ATLANTIC OCEAN

Gulf of Mexico

People per square mile
- >13,000
- 6,500-12,999
- 1,300-6,499
- 250-1,299
- 125-249
- 65-124
- 13-64
- 8-12
- 0-7

NATIVE AMERICANS

Indigenous population groups in North America include the Inuit, Aleut, Cherokee, Navajo, Chippewa, Sioux, and Pueblo. Their distribution is very uneven, and they are often less well-off economically than their white counterparts.

Native American students improve their IT skills at Spokane Indian Reservation, United States.

Originally, there were hundreds of Native American tribes. The size of the Native American population in 1500 has been disputed, with estimates ranging between 1.1 million and 12 million people. By 1900, however, the Native American population had fallen to only 237,000. The main cause of this genocide was disease, which accounted for up to 90 percent of the deaths. Native Americans had their own rich and varied cultures and traditions. They also made valuable contributions to white American society, for example by introducing early European settlers to crops, such as maize, beans, and squash, and sharing their knowledge of traditional medicines. Today, the United States is home to more than 2 million Native Americans, with about 800,000 living on reservations and 1.2 million residing in urban areas. The United States has approximately three hundred Federal Indian reservations and five hundred federally recognized tribes.

FACT FILE

One-third of foreign-born people in the United States live in the cities of Los Angeles, California, and New York.

MIGRATION AND IMMIGRATION

One of the key characteristics of North America's population is migration. Immigration into North America from countries outside the region is also important. The "brain drain" from Europe and Asia illustrates this trend. In 1961, 75 percent of Canada's immigrants came from Europe and 12 percent from the United States. By 2000, more than 50 percent of Canada's immigrants came from Asia. Highly qualified workers, such as doctors, are drawn to North America by the opportunity of well-paid jobs.

FACT FILE

Most of the people on fixed-term visas, which allow foreigners with technical qualifications to work in the United States, come from India.

Compared with its rich northern neighbor, Mexico has a relatively low standard of living, insufficient jobs, and poorer education and health systems. Estimates suggest that each year between one and two million Mexicans try to cross into the United States. Although illegal Mexican workers are a drain on U.S. social programs and benefits, they are essential to the nation's economy. The immigrants are willing to take harder, dirtier, seasonal, more monotonous, more dangerous, less-skilled, and lower-paid jobs. Despite the low pay by U.S. standards, some immigrants can earn more during three or four months in the United States than in a full year in Mexico. Within Mexico, most migrants have left the countryside to seek work in the cities. In turn, Mexico receives immigrants from its poorer neighbors to the south, such as El Salvador and Guatemala.

French is the official language in the Canadian province of Québec.

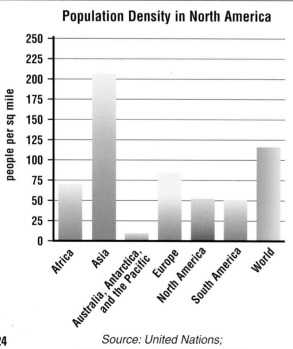

Population Density in North America

people per sq mile

Source: United Nations;
Britannica Book of the Year 2004

RACE AND ETHNICITY

More than 70 percent of North Americans are descendants of Europeans. More than one-third of the population of the United States, and nearly half the population of Canada, have ancestors from Great Britain. More than one-quarter of Canadians have French ancestors. In the United States, there is also a significant number of people from Germany, Italy, Poland, and eastern European and Scandinavian countries. The European ancestors of Central Americans mostly came from Spain.

African Americans make up 12 percent of the United States' population. They are largely descended from slaves who were brought over from Africa to work on plantations in the South. After the abolition of slavery in 1865, and throughout the twentieth century, many African Americans moved north in search of new opportunities and higher-paying jobs in cities, such as New York, Chicago, and Detroit.

Most of the people of the Caribbean islands are also descended from black Africans, but this varies between the islands. Although the native Caribs were almost completely wiped out by the early colonists, about three thousand Caribs still live on the east side of Dominica, and smaller populations of Caribs live on St. Vincent and Trinidad. Other people in the Caribbean are of mixed black and white descent. In Barbados and Montserrat, for example, live people who are descendants of Irish slaves or convicts who mixed with indigenous peoples.

Many of the people of Mexico and Central America are *mestizos*, people of mixed white and Native American ancestry. *Mestizos* account for about 50 percent of Central America's population and up to 90 percent of the population of El Salvador. The exception is Costa Rica, which has a predominantly white population. In contrast, Native Americans account for only 20 percent of the population of Central America, although 60 to 70 percent of Guatemala's population is Native American.

Asians make up a small but growing percentage of North America's population. In 2000, 4.3 percent of U.S. residents were Asian, an increase of 65 percent since 1990. Asians began emigrating to the continent in the 1800s and have come mainly from China, Japan, Korea, and the Philippines. A large concentration of Asians live in the states of Hawaii and California. More than two-thirds of Hawaii's population consists of "Pacific Island population"—nonwhite people, including Pacific islanders and those of Asian descent.

People from many different ethnic backgrounds have made their homes in the United States.

FACT FILE

In Belize, Honduras, and Guatemala, a distinct ethnic group—the Garifuna—is descended from Caribs and black slaves from Africa.

FACT FILE

There are only about 136,000 Inuits and Aleuts (people related to the Inuit) in North America. They live in Alaska, northern Canada, and Greenland.

The civil rights movement in the United States was a campaign for equal rights for black citizens that started in the mid-1950s. The most famous civil rights leader was Dr. Martin Luther King Jr. When the movement began, segregation laws in U.S. southern states separated black and white people in all areas of life, including in schools, in theaters, and on public transportation. Black people were treated like second-class citizens. After a long and bitter struggle, the Civil Rights Act was passed in 1964 forbidding segregation in public places. Black people gained equal voting rights the following year. Dr. King was assassinated in 1968. Despite legislation, racial discrimination and prejudice still exists among people in many parts of the United States, as well as in other parts of North America.

African Americans have fought long and hard for racial equality.

FACT FILE

The proportion of people living on less than US$2 per day in North America varies from 45 percent in El Salvador and 44.4 percent in Honduras, to 24.3 percent in Mexico, 14.3 percent in Costa Rica, and less than 2 percent in Cuba. (Figures for Canada and the United States are not recorded.)

QUALITY OF LIFE

The quality of life varies enormously across North America. Residents of Canada have the highest life expectancy in North America at 79 years. Average life expectancy is also high in the United States (76 years), Barbados (77 years), and Bermuda (77 years). In contrast, life expectancy in Haiti is only 53 years. High life expectancies are partly the result of good living conditions, such as clean water, proper sanitation, and sufficient food, and partly a result of government investment in health care. The United States spends 12.9 percent of its Gross Domestic Product (GDP) on health care, Canada 9.3 percent, and Honduras 8.6 percent. Poorer countries, such as Belize, Nicaragua, and Guatemala, cannot afford to invest such a large proportion of their GDP. Typically, the figure is between 2 and 3 percent for them.

The proportion of people with access to clean water varies from almost 100 percent in the United States, Canada, and Barbados, to 77 percent in Nicaragua and 46 percent in Haiti. Particular problem areas include shanty towns and rural areas. In Mexico, for examle, 95 percent of urban residents have access to clean water, but only 69 percent of rural people do.

Closely linked to water is the issue of sanitation. In Barbados, Canada, and the United States, 100 percent of the population has access to adequate sanitation. This number falls to 74 percent in Mexico, 50 percent in Belize, and 28 percent in Haiti. Fifty percent of Haiti's urban population benefits from adequate sanitation, but only 16 percent of its rural people. In Cuba, however, where the government has made a much larger investment in health and welfare, 99 percent of the urban population and 95 percent of the rural population have access to sanitation.

Not everyone has private access to clean water. This man is using public washing facilities in a street in Cozumel, Mexico.

URBAN VERSUS RURAL

Many of the smaller countries in North America are still largely rural, while the more developed countries have higher levels of urbanization, meaning a large proportion of people live in urban areas. Some Caribbean islands, however, have quickly increasing rates of urbanization. Across Central America and the Caribbean, the proportion of people living in urban areas ranges from 40 percent in Guatemala to more than 95 percent in Puerto Rico and Guadeloupe. In general, the proportion of people living in urban areas is increasing rapidly. In 1940, only 35 percent

FACT FILE

In New York, the average daily water consumption is 118 gallons (448 liters) per person. In Cuidad Juarez, Mexico, it is 89 gallons (336 liters) per person, while in Havana, Cuba, it is only 26 gallons (100 liters) per person.

of Mexico's population lived in urban areas. By 2001, this number had more than doubled to 74.6 percent.

Rural communities in North America range from small, isolated communities in Nunavut, Canada, to densely populated lowlands on Caribbean islands, such as Antigua. Most rural areas were traditionally associated with farming, but many are now becoming involved in services, including tourism, with residents commuting to nearby urban areas for work. The decline in farm work is partly due to increased use of machinery in farming, which has lowered the demand for labor, but it is also a result of the low wages traditionally paid to farm workers.

About 75 percent of the U.S. population lives in cities and large towns. Many cities are so large that they have grown together with neighboring suburbs and cities to form large metropolitan areas. New York is a good example of such an area. The city itself is made up of five boroughs—Brooklyn, the Bronx, Manhattan, Staten Island, and Queens—each of which is also a county of New York state. Beyond its city limits, the New York metropolitan area includes numerous cities and towns in neighboring Long Island and other parts of New York state, and

FACT FILE

Since 1970, levels of urbanization have increased rapidly in Honduras, from 29 percent in 1970 to 45.6 percent in 2003.

A busy Fifth Avenue in New York City. The northeastern United States is an area of very high population density.

even parts of New Jersey and Connecticut. Some multiple metropolitan areas with economic and transportation links, or those that have physically grown together, are considered one continuous megalopolis, or densely populated region, even across state lines. East Coast cities from Boston to Washington, for example, are often described as forming one huge megalopolis.

URBAN DEVELOPMENT

Urban development has reached massive proportions in parts of North America. One consequence of this growth has been that large cities, such as Mexico City and Los Angeles, now have a major problem with traffic congestion and pollution from vehicle emissions. Population growth in smaller urban areas is also significant. Between 1975 and 2000, for example, the population of the metropolitan area of Phoenix, Arizona, grew by more than 2 million people to 3.23 million. Phoenix's expansion is due to a number of factors, including a diverse economy, pleasant climate, good quality of life, and a relatively low cost of living—all of which have encouraged companies to relocate there. Such rapid growth leads to suburban sprawl, as cities expand rapidly around their edges to accommodate the influx of people.

The quality of life in urban areas is highly variable. In general, high-quality lifestyles in suburban areas contrast with the deprivation of ghettos and shanty towns in less developed parts of North America. Even in small cities, such as Castrie, St. Lucia, there is visible evidence of inequalities in standards of living. In the larger urban areas, hot spots of deprivation can be found in inner cities, such as Watts in central Los Angeles, and in shanty towns, such as Naucalpan, Ecatepec, and Netzahualcoyotl on the edge of Mexico City.

FACT FILE

One-fifth of the U.S. population lives on just one-fiftieth of the country's land, clustered in the area from Boston to Washington.

The rural, hillside community of San Mateo, Guatemala.

4. NORTH AMERICAN CULTURE AND RELIGION

MANY PEOPLE IN NORTH AMERICA HAVE STRONG RELIGIOUS BELIEFS. For many of the early European immigrants and later immigrants to North America, the promise of religious tolerance—particularly in the United States—was especially attractive.

FACT FILE

Ninety-seven percent of Christians in Central America, 47 percent in Canada, and 21 percent in the United States are Roman Catholic.

RELIGION IN NORTH AMERICA

In the United States today, more than 60 percent of people are Christian, and about 40 percent attend religious services regularly. Sixty million Roman Catholics and 100 million Protestants live in the United States. Protestant religions include a number of denominations, such as Baptist, Lutheran, the Society of Friends (Quaker), Amish, and Adventists. Other important religions include Judaism (6 million), Islam (6 million), Hinduism, and Buddhism. Two of the fastest-growing religions in the United States are the Church of Jesus Christ of Latter-day Saints (Mormons) and the Church of Christ, Scientist (Christian Scientists).

Large numbers of people with the same religious faith live in certain areas of the United States. Members of the Mormon Church, for example, account for 77 percent of the population in Utah and 27 percent in Idaho. They settled in Utah in the nineteenth century to escape from the opposition to their beliefs that they had encountered elsewhere. The so-called "Bible Belt"—an area of the United States that is home to many people with strong Protestant beliefs and a strict interpretation of the Bible—stretches across several southern and

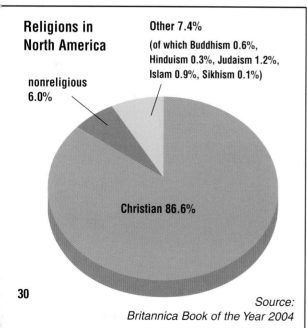

Religions in North America

Other 7.4%
(of which Buddhism 0.6%, Hinduism 0.3%, Judaism 1.2%, Islam 0.9%, Sikhism 0.1%)

nonreligious 6.0%

Christian 86.6%

Source: Britannica Book of the Year 2004

midwestern states. Baptists form the majority of the Christian population in Mississippi, Alabama, and Georgia. Large numbers of Roman Catholics live in areas associated with Irish immigration, such as the northern cities of New York, Boston, and Chicago, and more recently with areas of Latino immigration, including southern Florida and California. On a much smaller scale, many Amish live in Pennsylvania.

In Canada, the Roman Catholic Church, United Church of Canada, and Anglican churches have the largest following. More than 75 percent of Jews in Canada live in Toronto and Montreal, while members of the Presbyterian Church are centered in Ontario, and Canadian Baptists live primarily in the Maritime Provinces of the east coast. Roman Catholics mostly live in areas of French immigration, such as Québec.

Most countries in Central America are predominantly Roman Catholic. The Spanish conquistadors first brought Catholicism to the region and were closely followed by missionaries who worked to convert Native Americans to their religion. Belize, which came under British rather than Spanish influence, has been mainly Protestant, although the proportion of Catholics in Belize is increasing. Much of the black population along the Caribbean coast is Protestant, also a result of British colonialism. Many supporters of Rastafarianism also live in the Caribbean. Rastafarians believe that Haile Selassie, the former Emperor of Ethiopia, was the Messiah and that all believers will some day return to Ethiopia.

A Christian Holy Week procession in Guatemala.

Two men from Chichimila in Yucatán, Mexico, cook sacred foods during a rain ceremony.

The Green Bay Packers play the Washington Redskins in a National Football League game.

Some traditional Native American beliefs are still practiced in North America. In the past, for example, many Inuits were converted to Christianity, and their own religions were forbidden. Today, some Inuits have returned to their ancient practices and beliefs. Similarly, in parts of Central America, indigenous populations, such as the Maya, continue to hold traditional beliefs—for example, worship of the Rain God. Some islanders in the eastern Caribbean believe in *obeah*, a type of black magic used to cast spells on an enemy. Obeah uses magical rituals to contact supernatural forces.

SPORTS

The United States is particularly known for baseball, basketball, and football. Baseball is based on the English game rounders. The World Series was first held in 1903 between the winners of the two professional baseball leagues in the United States, now known as the National League and the American League. Football is probably the most popular spectator sport, with about 90 million people watching the Super Bowl Championship alone. In Canada, popular winter sports include skiing, skating, and ice hockey—which was invented in Montreal in 1835. The game of lacrosse was developed in Canada from a Native American game called *baggatway*. In addition, many Canadian teams, such as the Toronto Blue Jays, play baseball in the U.S.-based major leagues.

Soccer is the most popular sport in Mexico and, indeed, throughout Central America. The World Cup was hosted by Mexico in 1970 and by the United States in 1994. Basketball also has a big following in Mexico, as well as other sports that are Spanish in origin, such as bullfighting, rodeo, and *jai alai.* Jai alai is a fast ball game, based on the Spanish game *pelota*, in which two, four, or six players use long, curved wicker baskets to hit a ball—the *pelota*—inside a walled court.

Informal games of cricket are a very familiar sight in the Caribbean.

In parts of the Caribbean, cricket is extremely popular. It was introduced to the region by British colonists and is a bat-and-ball game played between two teams of eleven players. The West Indies cricket team is made up of players from all over the Caribbean, and the Test Matches (games against other countries) are played on cricket pitches, or grounds, in Trinidad, Antigua, St. Lucia, Barbados, and Jamaica. Famous cricketers include Sir Garfield "Gary" Sobers and Brian Lara.

Recreational water sports are also important, especially in the Caribbean and along the coastlines and on the lakes of the United States. Sailing, windsurfing, scuba diving, and swimming are popular among tourists as well as local people.

North America has produced many world-class, Olympic athletes. including Carl Lewis (a sprinter and long jumper who won nine gold medals in four Olympic Games) and Mark Spitz (who won a record seven gold medals for swimming in the 1972 Munich Olympics). Famous Jamaican sprinters include Marlene Ottey and Lennox Miller. Cubans, such as Felix Savon, dominated Olympic boxing during the 1990s. Donovan Bailey, a Canadian track star, is one of the many sports personalities who has made a successful transition from the sports field into sports management.

FACT FILE

In terms of employment, the sports industry in the United States is larger than film, radio, television, and education combined. It accounts for more than 2.3 million jobs and US$48 billion in wages and salaries.

FACT FILE

At the 2004 Olympics in Athens, the United States won thirty-five gold medals, Cuba nine, Canada three, and the Bahamas one.

The most famous of all reggae singers was Bob Marley, seen here in performance in 1980. Reggae musicians often sing about social conditions because their music developed as a form of protest against various discriminations they faced.

MUSIC

The Caribbean has a very rich musical heritage, with its roots in Africa, Spain, France, England, and Ireland. Calypso originated in the eighteenth century in Trinidad as satirical songs sung in French by slaves working on plantations. Modern calypso has sharp political and social messages. Well known calypso artists include the Mighty Sparrow, David Rudder, and Winston "Gypsy" Peters. Similarly, blues music in the United States grew from the songs that slaves sang on plantations. Blues was very important in the development of jazz, and it had a huge influence on popular music and rock 'n' roll during the twentieth century in the United States.

Ska evolved in Jamaica in the 1950s. It is a blend of calypso, rhythm and blues, and African-Jamaican folk music. Similarly, reggae is a blend of ska, blues, calypso, and rock. Many of the songs are born out of social protest and were popularized by the late Bob Marley. In contrast, *zonk* originated in the French West Indies and is a mix of African and French dance music.

A TV CONTINENT

There are more than one thousand television stations in North America, although most are local channels that are usually affiliates (smaller associates) of national broadcast networks. Americans have more choices in their television viewing than anyone else in the world. Many channels—particularly cable channels—are dedicated to providing a single type of programming, such as sports, educational, news, movies, or entertainment. Many programs, such as *Friends* or *The Simpsons*, have become popular worldwide.

THE CAR

The automobile is an integral part of North American culture. The United States has more cars per person than any other country in North America, with 481 cars per thousand people (ranked twelfth in the world), whereas Haiti has the lowest ratio at 4.4 cars per thousand people. Within the United States, up to 90 percent of trips made between towns and cities are taken in cars. Increased ownership of cars has allowed cities to spread out—a process known as urban sprawl. The trend toward bigger "gas-guzzling" sports utility vehicles (SUVs) in recent years is a serious environmental issue in the United States. In Mexico City, emissions from 3.5 million vehicles help produce some of the most polluted air in the world.

FOOD

Fast food is another feature of North American culture, mainly in the United States but also in Canada and increasingly in Mexico. While fast food has contributed to a rise in obesity in the United States and Mexico, other factors, such as sedentary lifestyles, changes in diet, and an increase in the size of food portions, are also to blame for this unhealthy trend. As a result of the many different peoples who settled in the United States, such as Italian, Mexican, and Chinese, a wide variety of ethnic food is available in restaurants in even the smallest towns across the country. The United States is also a country of meat eaters—particularly beef.

Detroit, Michigan, is one of the most important regions of car manufacturing in the world. Its annual International Auto Show (*above*) is a showcase for and promotes the sales of new cars.

FACT FILE

Up to seven million new vehicles are bought every year in the United States.

FACT FILE

The United States has the longest road network in the world— 3,917,425 miles (6,304,193 km).

5. NATURAL RESOURCES IN NORTH AMERICA

NORTH AMERICA, IN PARTICULAR THE UNITED STATES, is a continent rich in natural resources.

OIL AND NATURAL GAS

In the United States, oil and natural gas are found in Alaska, the Gulf states of Texas and Louisiana, Oklahoma, California, Pennsylvania, and Kentucky. In Canada, oil and gas reserves in Alberta supply 50 percent of the country's oil and 90 percent of its natural gas requirements.

Mexico is one of the largest oil-exporting nations outside OPEC—the Organization of Petroleum Exporting Countries, which is made up mainly of oil-producing countries in the Middle East. In 2003, Mexico achieved an output of 3.8 million barrels of oil per day (the main OPEC countries produce about 24 million barrels of oil per day). Most of the production comes from the Gulf of Mexico. Trinidad also exports natural gas and oil, mainly to the United States, and has major petrochemical industries.

COAL

The western United States has huge reserves of coal. Most of the coal mining is done by strip mining, in which the surface layer is removed and the exposed coal then mined. This type of mining, however, has a dramatic effect on the environment by removing

A quarry in Pennsylvania. The environmental effects of strip mining are serious as well as visually unattractive.

Energy planners are eager to develop the vast oil resources that exist in Alaska. Alaskan oil provides nearly one-third of the total oil reserves in the United States and one-eighth of its total natural gas reserves. Those in favor of development claim that most Alaskans see oil as their main source of jobs and wealth in the future.

Some Native American groups, however, claim they would prefer to live in their traditional way rather than benefit from oil income. In northern Alaska, the seven thousand people of the Gwich'in Nation consider the coastal plain of the Arctic Refuge sacred because it is the calving ground for the porcupine caribou herd. The subsistence lifestyle of the Gwich'in is intimately bound to this herd for food, clothing, and tools made from caribou antlers and bone. As a result, the Gwich'in vigorously oppose any oil development in the region.

Part of the operation to cleanup oil spilled from the tanker the *Exxon Valdez* after it ran aground in Prince William Sound, Alaska, in 1989. About 11 million gallons (42 million liters) of oil polluted 1,300 miles (2,100 km) of the Alaskan shoreline.

natural vegetation, reducing biodiversity, and ruining the landscape. In West Virginia, for example, strip mining at Pigeonroost Hollow has destroyed much of the natural forest and wildlife. Canada also has important coal reserves, and a large proportion of the coal mined in British Columbia is exported to Japan. Fossil fuels account for over 75 percent of Mexico's energy production.

FACT FILE

The United States has 550 billion tons (500 billion tonnes) of coal—enough to last three hundred years.

Hydroelectric power on the Kootenay River, British Columbia, Canada. HEP has great potential in many parts of North America.

HYDROELECTRIC POWER

Hydroelectric power (HEP) is very important in Canada. It accounts for nearly 66 percent of Canada's electricity generation and 97 percent of the country's renewable electricity generation. The largest HEP plant in Canada is located at James Bay in Québec. Canada exports electricity to the United States, as well as crude petroleum and natural gas. HEP supplies almost 15 percent of Mexico's electricity production. The mountainous landscapes of Central America have many narrow, steep river valleys that are relatively easy to dam. Combined with high rainfall and high water levels, these dams provide a plentiful supply of HEP for Central American countries.

RENEWABLE ENERGY

A number of projects serve as examples of using other forms of renewable energy. In Belize, for example, electricity is generated by burning biomass (biodegradable material, such as sawdust), and solar power is used to generate electricity and heat water in health clinics. In Honduras, biomass (sugar cane waste pulp) is also used for the generation of electricity at Tres Valles. Nicaragua uses solar energy for health clinics, while Panama has developed a solar water-pumping system for farms as well as using solar power in its national parks to provide energy for research stations and tourist camps.

Both the United States and Mexico have considerable potential for geothermal energy—tapping heat from the interior of the earth to produce energy. The production of geothermal energy in the United States has declined in recent years, however, due to overexploitation of the giant Geysers steam field in California. As water is taken out of the geyser reservoir, the pressure in the reservoir drops, making it more difficult and costly to extract water and causing a gradual decline in levels of productivity. In Mexico, Costa Rica, El Salvador, and Guatemala, money is being invested in geothermal energy, and capacity has substantially increased in recent years.

The Honduran government has brought solar energy to many remote and isolated towns, such as here at San Ramon Centro, where solar energy powers the school's computer center.

MINERALS

Mineral resources are widespread throughout North America. Canada is the world's leading producer of nickel, zinc, uranium, and potash. It is also a major producer of cobalt, gypsum, and asbestos. Mexico is the world's leading producer of silver. In some countries, such as Haiti, mineral resources exist (including gold, copper, and bauxite) but are not mined, mainly as a result of political upheavals during the last forty years. Jamaica has large reserves of bauxite, which is the raw material used to produce aluminum. In the 1970s, production was mostly controlled by foreign companies, but more recently, the government has imposed a levy, or tax, on bauxite production so that more of the benefits will return directly to Jamaica.

FACT FILE

Trinidad is the most resource-rich island in the Caribbean, with oil, asphalt, and natural gas. Fossil fuels account for 99.8 percent of its energy production.

FORESTRY

Important timber resources exist in the Rockies, the Pacific Northwest (Oregon and Washington), and in Alaska. Forests cover more than 40 percent of Canada, and about half of them

Forestry is an important part of the economy in large parts of Canada.

are commercially operated. Most of the trees cut in Canada are softwood, coniferous trees. Canada is the world's largest producer of newspaper, the second largest producer of wood pulp, and the third largest producer of sawn timber. Forestry is also important in Central America. In some places, however, deforestation has become a major problem. Many of the rain forests of Central America have been cut down to make space for farmland. In Panama, large-scale deforestation is leading to serious soil erosion, which in turn is causing the Panama Canal to fill with silt. If this problem is not addressed, the movement of ships through the canal between the Atlantic and Pacific oceans could be affected.

FARMING

North America is ranked third behind Asia and Europe in farming production. It produces approximately 60 percent of the world's soybeans and 50 percent of the world's maize and sorghum. It also produces about 25 percent of the world's citrus fruits and oats.

Farming benefits from the deep, fertile, black earth in the midwestern United States. The Great Plains of Canada and the United States are major wheat-growing regions. In the drier western and southwestern regions, irrigation is used to produce alfalfa, cotton, and sugar. Wheat, beans, and maize are important crops grown in Mexico, while in tropical parts of Central America and the Caribbean, coffee and bananas are vital crops.

The rich soils in Central America support a thriving farming system. The mountainous terrain limits production in many areas, however, although terraces—artificial steps cut into the steep slopes—are used to grow crops in places such as Montserrat and St. Lucia. Farming accounts for a large percentage of exports in these countries. In 2002, for example, exports of bananas and sugar were worth nearly US$3 billion for the economy of Guatemala and almost US$1.3 billion for Honduras.

FISHING

About 25 percent of the world's annual fish catch comes from the North Atlantic Ocean between Newfoundland and New England. The Gulf of Mexico is important for menhaden (used for fertilizer and fishmeal), shrimp, and lobsters. The main species caught in the Bering Sea, the Gulf of Alaska, and the Northern Pacific include pollock, sardines, mackerel, and anchovies. Salmon is an important catch in the Pacific waters of Canada and Alaska, but overfishing has reduced stocks in British Columbia, Alaska, and Washington state. In British Columbia, salmon are now raised in fish farms. Likewise, the cod fisheries in the Atlantic Ocean have nearly disappeared. As a result, both the Canadian and U.S. governments have placed restrictions on fishing in some waters.

FACT FILE

Up to 80 percent of commercially valuable fish populations in U.S. fisheries are already fully exploited or over-exploited.

FACT FILE

In 1992, Canada's cod industry collapsed due to overfishing, leading to the loss of forty thousand jobs. Fishing remains perilous despite a C$3.9 billion Fisheries and Adjustment Plan to revitalize the industry.

Catching salmon off the Alaskan coast. Fishing remains an important source of employment and income for many coastal and river communities.

6. THE NORTH AMERICAN ECONOMY

*T*HE ECONOMY OF NORTH AMERICA IS THE THIRD LARGEST IN THE world behind Europe and Asia. It continues to expand and grew by more than 2 percent in 2002. It benefits from a vast array of natural resources as well as a large and wealthy market. It also has a strong high-tech base, including research and development.

FACT FILE

The United States has the world's largest industrial output, worth US$2,684 billion in 2003. Canada was ninth, with an industrial output worth US$190 billion.

Silicon Valley—the home of high-technology industry in California.

THE UNITED STATES

The U.S. economy is a market-oriented economy, which means that private individuals and business firms make most of the decisions. Many of these companies are extremely large and deal with suppliers and customers around the world. Large numbers of multinational companies were founded and have their headquarters in the United States, including Microsoft Corporation, Ford Motor Company, and General Motors.

There are two main contrasting economic zones within the United States. The *rust belt* refers to the older, industrial regions of the northeastern and north central United States, which were based around manufacturing jobs, coal, iron, and steel. The *sunbelt* refers to regions in the south and southwest, from Florida to California, that have attracted industries that do not need to be located close to a raw material, including electronics and software companies, such as Dell Computers in Texas and Motorola in Phoenix. Many high-tech companies are located in California's so-called "Silicon Valley," about 50 miles (80 km) south of San Francisco.

High-tech industries are found elsewhere, too. Microsoft Corporation, for example, is based in Seattle.

Many U.S. companies have moved jobs out of the United States to benefit from cheap foreign labor and advantageous taxes. Examples include call-centers in Jamaica, the *maquiladoras* (industries that pay very low wages to produce goods cheaply) in Mexico, and Operation Bootstrap—a program of government support for industry through tax breaks—in the U.S. territory of Puerto Rico. Much of this outsourcing has gone to Asia, however, where the Indian software industry has taken over work that was previously carried out in the United States.

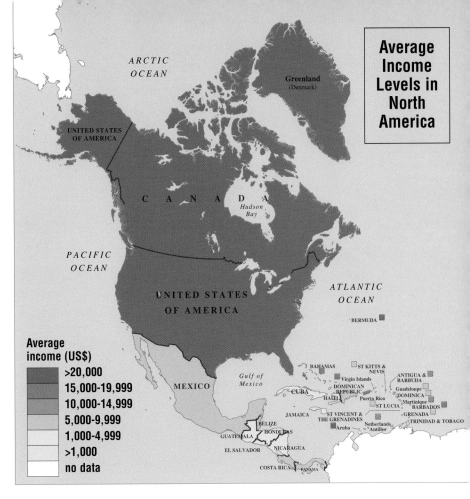

Average Income Levels in North America

Average income (US$)
- >20,000
- 15,000-19,999
- 10,000-14,999
- 5,000-9,999
- 1,000-4,999
- >1,000
- no data

CANADA

Canada is an affluent, high-tech, industrial society. Since World War II, Canada has been transformed from a largely rural economy into one that is primarily industrial and urban. Both the 1989 U.S.-Canada Free Trade Agreement (FTA) and the 1994 North American Free Trade Agreement (NAFTA) between the United States, Canada, and Mexico led to a huge increase in trade and economic integration with the United States. Canada does face one major problem, however—the southward migration to the United States of professionals lured by the prospect of higher pay and lower taxes.

FACT FILE

With worldwide sales of more than $237.1 billion, U.S. company ExxonMobil is ranked second among the world's largest companies. Its sales are greater than the GDP of Sweden or Turkey.

Many jobs have been moved from the United States to other parts of North America where wages are lower, such as the jobs found in the *maquiladoras* industries on the U.S.-Mexico border.

MEXICO

Although Mexico has substantial energy and mineral resources, it has not fully developed its economy. Population growth is faster than the growth of jobs, and the agricultural sector is weak. Most of the manufacturing in Mexico occurs in and around Mexico City and along the U.S.-Mexican border in maquiladoras, or assembly factories. Income distribution in Mexico remains highly unbalanced—the richest 10 percent of households receive 41 percent of the national income, and the poorest 10 percent of all households receive just 1.6 percent.

TRADE AGREEMENTS

A number of trade agreements between various countries in North America have worked to open up each other's markets. The North American Free Trade Agreement (NAFTA) between Mexico, Canada, and the United States allows free trade between the three countries. Mexico's trade with the United States and Canada has tripled since the implementation of NAFTA in 1994. Mexico has also signed free-trade agreements with Guatemala, Honduras, El Salvador, and the European Free Trade Association (Iceland, Norway, Switzerland, and Liechtenstein), putting more than 90 percent of Mexico's trade under such agreements. Some people argue that NAFTA allows U.S. companies to exploit cheap labor in Mexico, as well as giving them increased access to new markets. Others say that thousands of high-paying manufacturing jobs have been lost in the United States because lower labor costs in Mexico have led companies to move jobs south of the border.

In 2004, the United States, Costa Rica, El Salvador, Guatemala, Honduras, and Nicaragua signed the Central American Free Trade Agreement (CAFTA). Under CAFTA, tariffs have been removed to increase the amount of trade between the United States and the Central American countries. Critics of CAFTA argue that the agreement could make poverty worse in Central America because it allows the export of staple products, such as rice, maize, and beans from the United States. These crops are heavily subsidized in the United States, and if farmers in other CAFTA countries are unable to compete with the low prices, their livelihoods may be threatened as a result.

The Central America Common Market (CACM) was established in 1961 by El Salvador, Guatemala, Honduras, and Nicaragua. Costa Rica joined in 1962. The aim of CACM is to foster economic development and cooperation between the smaller countries of Central America and to attract industrial investment. Despite problems due to political instability in some countries, CACM has been reasonably successful at lowering trade barriers between its member countries.

HONDURAS

Honduras is one of the poorest countries in the Western hemisphere with an extraordinarily unequal distribution of income. It is hoping for expanded trade opportunities under the Enhanced Caribbean Basin Initiative to improve trade and economic opportunities, and it is also looking for aid as part of the Heavily Indebted Poor Countries (HIPC) initiative. Growth remains dependent, however, on the status of the U.S. economy (Honduras' major trading partner), on prices of major commodities, such as coffee, and on the reduction of the high crime rate.

FACT FILE

In Honduras, the richest 10 percent of households receive 43 percent of the country's income, while the poorest 10 percent receive only 0.6 percent. More than 40 percent of the population survives on less than US$2 per day.

Washing bananas at a plantation in San Pedro Sula, Honduras. Many jobs in farming are low-paid and unskilled.

DEBT

Debt is widespread in North America. Debt repayments (as a percentage of exports of goods and services) are as high as 24.5 percent in Belize and 22.2 percent in Nicaragua. In practical terms, this debt burden means that a poor country may be paying out more in debt service, or interest, payments than it can afford to spend on vital services, such as health and education. Nevertheless, in the 1990s, Mexico managed to reduce its debt burden from 18.3 percent to 14.1 percent, while Jamaica's debt has fallen from 27 percent to 16.8 percent. Many of the Caribbean islands, such as the Dominican Republic, Grenada, Haiti, St. Vincent, and Trinidad and Tobago, have a debt burden of below 10 percent. Some countries with great poverty and high debt burdens, such as Honduras and Nicaragua, are receiving aid under a program run by the World Bank—the Heavily Indebted Poor Countries (HIPC) Initiative. This program aims to provide debt relief in return for sound economic policies and measures to reduce poverty.

THE CARIBBEAN

The Caribbean Community and Common Market (CARICOM) was established in 1973 to promote economic development across the Caribbean. CARICOM also makes policies covering a wide range of issues, from health to the environment. Nevertheless, the economies of many Caribbean islands remain vulnerable. Many are highly dependent on tourism for income. Bahamas, Barbados, and St. Lucia, for example, all earn more than one-third of their GDP from tourism. In Antigua, tourism accounts for more than half of its GDP, and low tourist numbers since early 2000 have slowed Antigua's economy.

Despite its reliance on tourism, the economy of St. Lucia is one of the more stable

Harvesting sugar cane in Barbados. Farming has been mechanized in many Caribbean countries.

in the Caribbean. St. Lucia has been able to attract foreign business and investment, especially in its offshore banking and tourism industries. Its manufacturing sector is the most diverse in the eastern Caribbean area, and the St. Lucian government is trying to revitalize the banana industry. St. Lucia's manufacturing base is varied, including plastics and textiles, coconut products, cigarettes, rum, mineral water, toys, cardboard cartons, and electronic components.

Similarly, the economy of Barbados has been dependent on sugarcane cultivation and related activities, but in recent years it has diversified into manufacturing and tourism. Today, 15 percent of the workforce is employed in manufacturing and 75 percent in services, including tourism, offshore finance, and information services.

FACT FILE

In 2004, the Caribbean region attracted 22 million tourists, the United States had 50.89 million, and Mexico 20.64 million.

• • • • • • ▶ IN FOCUS: Small island economies

Small island economies face a number of issues. Their size means they have a small home market (Dominica has a population of only 79,000, and Barbados has only 270,000 people). A limited variety of natural resources and often a shortage of skilled labor are other hurdles to overcome. Many islands are remote, such as Barbados or Montserrat, causing increased transportation costs. Hurricanes are an additional problem in the Caribbean. Nevertheless, being surrounded by water and having a tropical climate provide the ideal conditions for coastal tourism. The insularity encouraged by island-living may also strengthen cultural and social identities—for example, calypso and reggae being associated with places such as Jamaica and Trinidad.

Tourists visit the Caribbean to enjoy its sunny skies, beautiful beaches, and clear waters.

7. NORTH AMERICA IN THE WORLD

NORTH AMERICA IS AN IMPORTANT GLOBAL REGION IN BOTH economic and political terms. The United States, in particular, has a vital role as the world's only superpower, following the collapse of the Soviet Union in 1991.

THE UNITED STATES

Even before it became the only superpower, the United States took a lead role in global affairs. After World War II ended, it helped to rebuild a war-devastated Europe and to oversee the foundation of major global institutions, such as the United Nations (UN), the World Bank, and the International Monetary Fund. These institutions all have their headquarters in the United States today. Another key role for the United States has been as a global mediator in regions of conflict, such as the former Yugoslavia and Israel. Indeed, it has a long history of attempting to bring about peace agreements between Israel and its Arab neighbors. When Iraq invaded Kuwait in 1991, however, the United States and its allies responded with the Gulf War. This role as "global policeman" has continued in the twenty-first century, with the United States leading a war in Iraq in 2003.

A U.S. soldier speaks to an Iraqi voter during the elections held in January 2005. In many places, people waited in line for hours in order to vote.

Since the terrorist attacks of September, 11, 2001 (9/11), the United States has collaborated with other North American and worldwide partners in the fight against terrorist activities. Under President George W. Bush, the United States has led the search for Osama bin Laden and the fight against al-Qaeda (the man and organization behind the

9/11 attacks), the attack on Afghanistan (the country which had provided support for al-Qaeda and in which bin Laden was believed to be living), and the defeat of the Taliban regime (the political leaders of Afghanistan). In the 2003 war, U.S. troops overthrew the regime of Iraqi dictator, Saddam Hussein. Since that time, largely U.S. and British peacekeeping forces have tried to control the escalating violence in Iraq. Democratic elections for a new Iraqi government took place in January 2005.

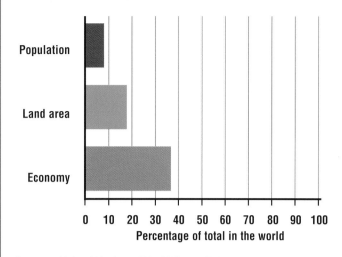

North America Compared with the Rest of the World

Bar chart showing Population, Land area, and Economy as a Percentage of total in the world (0 to 100).

Source: United Nations; World Bank; Britannica Book of the Year 2004

CANADA

Canada's most important international relationship in terms of trade is with the United States, accounting for 77 percent of Canada's exports and 65 percent of its imports. A number of disagreements exist between the two countries, however, including disputes about the levels of pollution given off by U.S. businesses close to the Canadian border. Traditionally, the main focus of trade for Canada was with Western Europe, but today most of Canada's trade is with Pacific Rim countries (including the United States), where new markets are emerging and economic growth is rapidly increasing.

In recent years, the focus of Canadian aid has switched from West Africa to Southeast Asia and eastern European countries, with particular emphasis on health, education, and child protection. Canadian troops have also been involved in recent (UN) peacekeeping operations, including those in Afghanistan, Somalia, and the former Yugoslavia.

FACT FILE

Canada gives more than twice as much government aid to foreign countries in relation to its GDP than the United States does: 0.25 percent of GDP compared to 0.1 percent in the United States.

A Canadian soldier patrols the streets of Mitrovicia, Kosovo, in 2000.

MEXICO

Mexico's main trade relationship is with the United States, and the signing of NAFTA has made it stronger. Mexico's close ties with its northern neighbor, and the processes of modernization and development put in place by its government, have resulted in Mexico having less in common with its poorer neighbors to the south. Nevertheless, Mexico has played an important role mediating conflicts in El Salvador, Guatemala, and Nicaragua.

PANAMA

Panama is another country that is trying to balance its relationship with the United States and its credibility with its neighbors. Panama received US$8.3 million in aid from the United States in 2004 and is expected to enter a free trade arrangement with the United States shortly. Ever since the construction of the Panama Canal, the United States has been involved in Panama's internal affairs. During the 1980s, an army general named Manuel Noriega became very influential in Panama. After a disputed election in 1989, Noriega seized power in Panama, declaring himself head of state. U.S. president George H.W. Bush sent troops into Panama to overthrow Noriega, who eventually surrendered. Noriega was imprisoned in the United States for drug trafficking offenses. Since that time, Panama has had a succession of civilian governments, and in 1999, the United States handed over control of the Panama Canal to Panama for the first time since its construction.

FACT FILE

The Panama Canal, which opened in 1914, is crucial to trade in the region. The canal saves 3,000 miles (4,800 km) in the journey from the eastern seaboard of the United States to its Pacific coast.

Manual Noriega with supporters in Panama City in 1989, before his arrest by U.S. forces.

CARIBBEAN

Most Caribbean countries retain strong ties with their former colonial powers. Antigua and St. Lucia, for example, have close economic, social, and political ties with the U.K. Many Caribbean countries have trade deals with the European Union to provide agricultural products, such as bananas. The United States has complained about this arrangement, claiming that it is a violation of free trade and is unfair to the operations of U.S. companies in Central America, since they do not have the same preferential access to the European Union market.

CUBA

For much of the twentieth century, Cuba's main trading partner was the United States. By the 1950s, approximately 65 percent of Cuba's exports and 75 percent of its imports were with the United States. Following the revolution that brought Fidel Castro to power, however, Cuba's trade shifted to the former Soviet Union and the Communist countries of eastern Europe. When Communism collapsed in eastern Europe and the Soviet Union, Cuba was forced to seek new trading partners. With U.S. sanctions still in place today, Cuba mainly trades with Canada, China, the Netherlands, Russia, and Spain. Sugar remains the country's prime export, although nickel, citrus fruits, coffee, and tobacco are also exported. Tourism is increasingly important, with more than five million visitors a year to Cuba anticipated by 2010.

Street entertainment in Havana, Cuba's capital city, where a musical group plays traditional Cuban music outside Havana Cathedral. Tourism is the great economic hope for many countries in North America, including Cuba.

8. NORTH AMERICAN WILDLIFE

NORTH AMERICA IS HOME TO MANY WELL KNOWN ANIMALS, including alligators, bald eagles, bison (buffalo), caribou, grizzly bears, and cougars as well as species in tropical areas, such as manatees and leatherback turtles.

Caribou are just one of many migratory species that travel vast distances to reach their summer grazing ranges on the Alaskan tundra.

THE FAR NORTH

The Arctic and coniferous forests of northern Canada and Alaska provide habitats for caribou and wolves. Caribou are migratory and move northward in summer to feast on tundra vegetation. The deciduous forests of northeastern North America are home to a wide variety of mammals, including bears, deer, skunks, and squirrels. The twenty to thirty species of trees in these forests support a huge variety of insects (more than three hundred species of insects can live on an oak tree), offering a wide range of food for a large variety of mammals. In contrast, the trees of the northern coniferous forests support only one to two species per acre (hectare) of trees. In turn, this restricted food supply means fewer species of birds and mammals live here. Typical species in these forests include moose, beavers, and timber wolves.

THE DRY LANDS

Deserts are normally considered barren areas, but North American deserts offer habitats to more than one hundred species of birds and more than forty species of mammals. Desert birds include roadrunners and burrowing owls, which live in the abandoned burrows of prairie dogs. Small mammals include ground squirrels and kangaroo rats, and mountain lions, rattlesnakes, and coyotes also live in this dry environment. Most desert mammals are very efficient in their use of water and generally take in enough moisture from their main food source.

GRASSLANDS

The grasslands of the Great Plains of the United States and Canada were once dominated by large numbers of just a few species of mammals. The Great Plains were home to vast numbers of bison and pronghorn antelope. Bison were brought to the edge of extinction in the mid- to late-nineteenth century. Thirty to sixty million bison once roamed the plains, but now only 250,000 to 350,000 can be found, mostly in private herds in protected areas. Smaller mammals include prairie dogs, which live in underground colonies that normally contain hundreds of individual animals at densities of up 1,550 per square mile (600 per sq km). Predators of the prairie dog include coyotes, prairie falcons, and burrowing owls.

ENDANGERED HABITATS

Some wildlife habitats are disappearing fast, largely due to urbanization and farming. Only 10 percent of North America's prairies remain as grassland —71 percent has been converted to cropland, and 19 percent has been

Prairie dogs are very social animals.

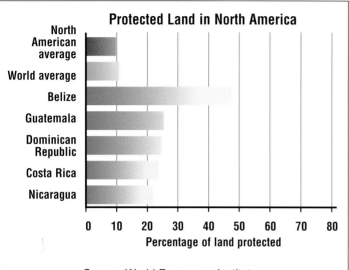

Protected Land in North America

Source: World Resources Institute

settled. Other developments, such as tourism and leisure-related construction, are having negative impacts on vulnerable coastal, wetland, and mountainous areas. On many Caribbean islands, building for the tourist industry has had a detrimental effect on the environment. At Rodney Bay in St. Lucia, for example, natural vegetation has been cut away to make space for the construction of hotels and marinas.

The Florida Everglades is a unique wetland that supports a variety of reptiles, such as alligators; amphibians; and wading birds, such as flamingos and herons. A little less than half (47 percent) of the Everglades is protected as a national park. Large-scale drainage programs, however, have reduced the volume of water reaching the Everglades, while fertilizers and pesticides have contaminated some of the water that flows into the region.

FACT FILE

The Florida panther is a highly endangered species. In the 1990s, closely related panthers were brought to Florida from Texas, and successful breeding has since taken place in captivity. Increased protection of the environment may yet save the species.

FACT FILE

Most of Mexico's tropical rain forest has been destroyed, with only about 5 percent still remaining.

The Everglades in Florida is home to many semiaquatic reptile species, such as this alligator.

IN FOCUS: Biodiversity "hot spots"

Biodiversity means biological diversity, the variety of all forms of life on Earth—plants, animals, and microorganisms. *Hot spots* refers to small regions that have a high bio-diversity or an important ecological value —the islands of Hawaii and the cloud forests of Costa Rica are both good exam-ples because of the unique diversity of their species. In Costa Rica, the cloud forest is the habitat of more than 100 species of mammals, 400 species of birds, 120 species of reptiles and amphibians, and several thousand species of insects. Another ex-ample, the Klamath-Siskiyou temperate forest in Washington, contains 30 conifer species and 131 plants, including the Brewer spruce, Port Orford cedar, and the insect-eating cobra lily.

In many areas, environments are now protected to preserve their beauty, the plant and animal life they contain, and the tourist revenues they bring in. The Monteverde Cloud Forest in Costa Rica is an example of a successfully managed

ecotourism project. Ecotourism refers to tourism that respects the environment and the needs of local people. At Monteverde, tourist numbers have been limited to protect the cloud forest, and local people have benefited from their involvement in tourism—as hosts and farmers and by developing attractions, such as riding stables, local crafts, and butterfly farms. Up to one-quarter of Belize, including offshore areas, has been designated as a nature reserve in some form, including the Cockscomb Basin Wildlife Sanctuary and the Blue Hole National Park. Never-theless, these parks still experience pres-sures from tourism and from logging companies eager to exploit the tropical forests for wood and other products, such as gums, resins, and oils.

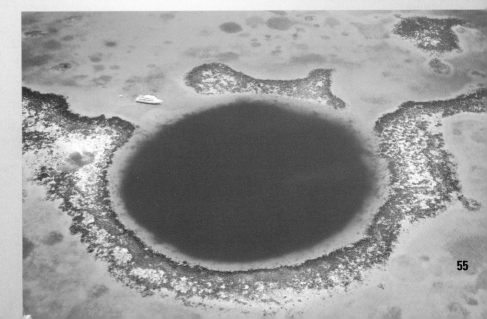

The Blue Hole is a sunken cave system surrounded by the Lighthouse Reef Atoll, off the coast of Belize.

FACT FILE

Coral off the coast of Montserrat has been killed by ash and dust emitted by the island's Soufriere Hills volcano.

FACT FILE

Florida's coral reefs attract annual tourism revenues of more than US$1.6 billion.

Coral reefs are often described as "the rain forests of the sea" because of their great biodiversity.

CORAL REEFS

Coral reefs are often thought of as "the rain forests of the sea" because of the huge number of species they contain and their vulnerability to destruction. Although coral reefs occupy less than 0.25 percent of the marine environment, they shelter more than 25 percent of all known fish species.

Coral reefs are another ecological hot spot and are experiencing severe pressures from modern development. Many of the Caribbean's coral reefs are threatened, with 29 percent of them, such as those off Belize, Montserrat, Antigua, Jamaica, and Puerto Rico, considered to be at high risk. Destruction takes many forms. If the water above a coral reef becomes cloudy, for example, the supply of light can be affected, which can kill the coral. This cloudiness can be caused by road construction that increases runoff, which carries sediment into the sea, by high levels of nutrients from agricultural areas, or by pollutants, such as petroleum products. Increased discharges of municipal waste also

decreases the the quality of water, killing coral in the process. Large sections of coral reefs have been destroyed by boats dropping anchors or running aground. Moreover, a desire for souvenirs from increasing numbers of tourists also increases the commercial exploitation of reefs.

The peaks of the Pitons in St. Lucia's Soufrière National Park are some of the most recognizable features in the Caribbean.

STRATEGIC PLANNING IN THE CARIBBEAN

Nearly all of the countries in the Caribbean have threatened ecosystems, and most have now developed plans to protect these environments. Nongovernment organizations (NGOs), including charities, are also increasingly involved in data collection and public education. In St Lucia, for example, the National Trust now incorporates scientific data in the management of its national parks, including the Barre de Isle rain forest and the Soufrière Marine Management Area. Similarly, Bermuda has closed its pot-fishing industry to protect the island's biodiversity and its lucrative reef-based tourism.

●●●●●●● ▷ IN FOCUS:
Folkestone Coral Reef, Barbados

The Folkestone Park and Marine Reserve was established in 1981 on the west coast of Barbados. The reserve stretches a total distance of 1.4 miles (2.2 km) and extends offshore a distance of 3,117 feet (950 m) at its widest point and 2,165 feet (660 m) at its narrowest. Within the reserve are four well-developed fringing reefs (coral reefs that grow in shallow waters), several patch reefs (small reefs), and an offshore bank reef (growing on deep bottom irregularities). But overfishing, poor habitat quality, and a severe disease that targeted reef fish in 1994 have all depleted the fish population. It is hoped that fish diversity will increase over time, although success has so far been slow.

9. THE FUTURE OF NORTH AMERICA

NORTH AMERICA IS LIKELY TO FACE MANY PROBLEMS IN THE future, and these vary across the continent. The physical environment provides many opportunities but also some problems. Tectonic activity in the Caribbean and the western edge of North America remains a real threat. The dangers of hurricane activity are increasing because more people are living in vulnerable areas. Low-lying coastal communities on the eastern side of subtropical North America are most at risk from this damage.

FACT FILE

Up to 30 percent of Mexico City's water is lost through leakage and theft by individuals and organized gangs, who sell it to those people without water.

WATER

In some areas, such as Mexico and the southwestern United States, water shortages may increase as weather patterns change and as population growth causes a strain on scarce water resources. Mexico City's main source of water, for example, is an aquifer, or water-bearing rock, which is running dry. Two-thirds of the city's water needs are supplied by this aquifer, with the rest coming from reservoirs 75 miles (120 km) away. Increasing demand on these distant water sources, however, is bringing Mexico City into conflict with neighboring states.

RESOURCES

Some natural resources, such as oil, will eventually run out and alternative forms of energy, such as HEP, solar, and geothermal energy, are being developed. These energy sources are important for the sustainable growth of North America. Other natural resources have been overexploited, with the fate of Canada's cod industry a good example. Nevertheless, the North American economy is large and strong and the immigration of skilled workers into North America, in particular to the United States, will provide it with an advantage over most other continents in terms of future research and development.

ECONOMIES

Cooperation between smaller nations is likely to increase in order to improve their trading options. Many smaller countries will try to vary their trading partners so that they are dealing with a range of countries in a variety of locations, such as Pacific Rim and European Union countries, as well as those within North America. More of the region's trade is likely to be with Asia, especially China.

For many of the Caribbean countries, dependence on tourism is likely to increase. In Antigua, employment in farming is declining, but employment in tourism is increasing. This shift may create advantages, such as investment and the growth of jobs, but it will require careful planning so that the disadvantages of environmental destruction, pollution, and economic dependence do not outweigh the advantages. Although it is a fine balancing act, tourism needs to be sustainable, as is the case in Costa Rica and Belize.

THE WORLD'S SUPERPOWER

In the United States, the continued battle against terrorism, both at home and overseas, is a major issue. As the world's only superpower, the United States will continue to find that other countries look to it for help. At the same time, many may blame the United States for some of their problems when things go wrong. The United States has a unique, and uniquely difficult, role in the world of the future.

The World Trade Center light memorial is a tribute to the thousands who died on 9/11 and a reminder of the work required in the years ahead if global peace is to be achieved.

STATISTICAL COMPENDIUM

Sources: UN Agencies, World Bank and Britannica

Nation	Area (sq miles)	Population (2003)	Urbanization (% population) 2003	Life expectancy at birth 2002 (in years)	GDP per capita (US$) 2002	Percentage of population under 15 years 2003	Percentage of population over 65 years 2003
Antigua and Barbuda	171	73,000	37.7	73.9	10,920	20	8
Aruba	74	100,000	45.4	N/A	N/A	N/A	N/A
Bahamas, The	5,380	314,000	89.5	67.1	17,280	28	6
Barbados	166	270,000	51.7	77.1	15,290	20	10
Belize	8,864	256,000	48.3	71.5	6,080	37	5
Bermuda	21	82,000	100.0	N/A	N/A	N/A	N/A
Canada	3,848,655	31,510,000	80.4	79.3	29,480	18	13
Costa Rica	19,725	4,173,000	60.6	78.0	8,840	30	6
Cuba	42,792	11,300,000	75.6	76.7	5,259	20	10
Dominica	290	79,000	72.0	73.1	5,640	25	8
Dominican Republic	18,787	8,745,000	59.3	66.7	6,640	32	5
El Salvador	8,122	6,515,000	59.6	70.6	4,890	35	5
Greenland	836,109	57,000	82.4	69.0	N/A	N/A	N/A
Grenada	133	80,000	40.7	65.3	7,280	34	8
Guadeloupe	687	440,000	99.7	N/A	N/A	N/A	N/A
Guatemala	42,031	12,347,000	46.3	65.7	4,080	42	3
Haiti	10,692	8,326,000	37.5	52.0	N/A	39	3
Honduras	43,422	6,941,000	45.6	68.8	2,600	41	3
Jamaica	4,243	2,651,000	52.1	75.6	3,980	30	7
Martinique	435	393,000	95.7	N/A	N/A	N/A	N/A
Mexico	755,866	103,457,000	75.5	73.3	8,970	32	5
Netherlands Antilles	309	221,000	69.7	76.0	N/A	23	9
Nicaragua	50,879	5,466,000	57.3	69.4	2,470	41	3
Panama	29,150	3,120,000	57.1	74.6	6,170	30	6
Puerto Rico	3,514	3,879,000	96.7	77.0	N/A	23	10
St. Kitts and Nevis	104	42,000	32.2	70.0	12,420	26	11
St. Lucia	238	149,000	30.5	72.4	5,300	31	6
St. Vincent and the Grenadines	150	120,000	58.3	74.0	5,460	27	8
Trinidad and Tobago	1,979	1,303,000	75.4	71.4	9,430	24	6
United States	3,794,085	294,043,000	80.1	77.0	35,750	21	12
Virgin Islands (U.S.)	136	111,000	93.6	78.0	N/A	25	9

GLOSSARY

biodiversity a measure of an environment's biological diversity based on the numbers of different species of plants and animals

biomass plant matter or other biodegradable material that can be used in various ways to make fuel

cash crop a crop that is grown for sale

civil rights movement a campaign of organized activities dedicated to winning equal rights and treatment for African American citizens

Commonwealth (British) an association of independent countries that were formerly part of the British Empire

Communism a system of government in which the government owns all or most property and controls the economy. It usually involves one-party, authoritarian rule.

conquistadors (**conquerors**) the early Spanish explorers and colonists who conquered large parts of Central America

cordillera a series of mountain ranges that run broadly parallel to each other and relate to a single mountain-formation period

Democracy a system of government in which representatives are chosen by the people in free elections

denomination a group within a religion that emphasizes a particular aspect of that faith

dictator an absolute, often oppressive ruler

ecosystem an integrated unit made up of plants, animals, and the environment in which they live

ecotourism the practice of visiting natural habitats in a way that minimizes the impact on the environment

El Niño a warm ocean current that periodically appears in the Pacific Ocean, disrupting the normal circulation and causing widespread climatic disorder, for example floods and droughts.

European Union (EU) a political and economic alliance of European countries

federal a system of government in which power is held by both national and regional governments

fossil fuels fuels such as coal, oil, and natural gas, formed from the fossilized remains of plants and animals that lived hundreds of millions of years ago

free trade unrestricted trade between countries without tariffs or other controls

genocide the deliberate and systematic murder of a specific group of people

geothermal energy derived from heat that is stored beneath Earth's surface

ghetto an area of a city, often densely populated and deprived, that is lived in by members of a minority

global warming the gradual warming of Earth's atmosphere, largely as a result of the burning of fossil fuels

Gross Domestic Product (GDP) the total earnings of a country from sources within that country, excluding earnings overseas

groundwater water that is held in porous rocks and soils in the ground

hydroelectric power (HEP) a type of energy generated by fast-flowing water moving through turbines

Ice Age a period of time in Earth's history when temperatures were lower and ice sheets covered more of Earth's surface

indigenous having originated in and living, growing, being produced, or occurring naturally in a particular area or environment, such as the native people of an area

Latino a person of Latin American origin, such as from Mexico, Central American, or the Caribbean, living in the United States

Maquiladoras foreign-owned factories in Mexico at which lower-paid workers assemble products for export

megalopolis a densely populated region that includes one or more large cities

permeable describes something that can be penetrated by liquid

pyroclastic flows clouds of superheated ash and gas from an erupting volcano

renewable energy power from sources that can is regenerative or will not run out

revenues the total income produced by a given source or earned by a business

Richter scale a scale for measuring the energy released by an earthquake

runoff water that flows over the ground rather than soaking into it

sanction a penalty imposed by one country against another

shanty town a poor area of a town or city where people live in flimsy dwellings, often without access to adequate sanitation

subsidy financial aid, often given by a government

superpower an extremely powerful nation country with great economic and political influence

tectonics the movement of Earth's crustal plates and the resulting effects, such as volcanic activity, earthquakes, and faults

tundra a treeless plain made up of grasses, sedge, heather, moss, and lichens, found at high latitudes and high altitudes

urbanization the quality or state of having the characteristics of urban areas; the proportion of people living in urban areas

FURTHER INFORMATION

BOOKS TO READ:

Berg, Elizabeth. *USA*. Countries of the World (series). Milwaukee: Gareth Stevens, 1999.

Blue, Rose and Corinne J. Naden. *Exploring Central America, Mexico, and the Caribbean*. Exploring the Americas (series). Chicago: Raintree, 2003.

Jermyn, Leslie. *Mexico*. Countries of the World (series). Milwaukee: Gareth Stevens, 1998.

Sakany, Lois. *Canada: A Primary Source Cultural Guide*. Primary Sources of World Cultures (series). New York: PowerPlus Books, 2004.

Walsh, Frank. *New York City*. Great Cities of the World (series). Milwaukee: World Almanac Library, 2004.

USEFUL WEB SITES:

www.geographia.com/
Explore the countries of Central America and the Caribbean on this informative site.

www.great-lakes.net/teach/
An educational site by the Great Lakes Commission about this important natural resource.

www.pbs.org/independentlens/newamericans/index.html
A PBS site about "The New Americans." Learn about the people who are immigrating to the melting pot of the United States in the twenty-first century.

www.welcome.topuertorico.org/
Learn more about the people, geography, history, economy, and culture of this U.S. territory.

Index

Page numbers in **bold** indicate pictures.

ABOUT THE AUTHOR

Dr. Garrett Nagle has written a number of geography textbooks and articles from primary school level to university level. He earned a doctorate from the University of Oxford, and he has taught in Oxford for the last twenty years, twelve of which were as Head of Geography.